LIFE and Love

Paul Jones

ISBN 978-1-950818-71-6 (paperback)

Copyright © 2020 by Paul Jones

All rights reserved. No part of this publication may be reproduced, distributed, or transmitted in any form or by any means, including photocopying, recording, or other electronic or mechanical methods without the prior written permission of the publisher. For permission requests, solicit the publisher via the address below.

Rushmore Press LLC
1 888 733 9607
www.rushmorepress.com

Printed in the United States of America

The poems you're about to read are about love and
the different situations we experience in life.

Life and Love

We've all have said it at some point in life and if you haven't
you probably will. We've all told someone that we love
them, but unfortunately many times in relationships, that
love turns out to be only lust. According to the bible, there
are for types of love. Eros, Storge, Phila and Agape.
Eros, is often the love a husband and a wife
demonstrates toward each other.
Storge, is family love the love mothers and fathers demonstrates
toward their children, and brothers and sisters.
Philia, is the love that two friends have for each
other. Yes, men you can tell each other's that you
love them without it meaning, Eros love.
Agape, Is the Love that God demonstrates toward mankind. John
3:16 For God so loved the world that he gave his only begotten son.
As you read these poems you will find, Life and Love.

I Hate You

In my mind I can say that I hate you
But in my heart, I know that this is untrue
Because every time that you walk out that door
I can truly say that my heart feels like it hits the floor
The words that I need to say I cannot find
But you're forever on my mind
How can my love for you be such a maybe
When you are the one who gave me my baby
When I look into your eyes,
You don't know how much happiness you bring
Sometime when I wake up, I ask myself is this all a dream
When you leave the house to do the things that you do
I know in my heart, that I'm going to miss you
When you get on the plane and it flies away
I pray that my love will bring you back this way
So, in my mind when I say that I hate you
I know in my heart that this is the wrong thing to do
In the house all the clocks and calendars I want to burn
As I wait so anxiously for your return
My mind might say that I hate you
But my heart and words always tell me that it's not true

Let's Do It Again

Because there's no sunshine when she's gone
But when she doesn't even have the decency to call home
Because I've been loving you way too long
For you to leave me and treat me so wrong
All I ask for is a little respect
But you continue to stomp on my heart, as if it was an insect
You say that you want to know if I care
I say just hold on baby, and I'll take you there
You once asked me to hold on until the midnight hour
Because you said that is when you get your power
You said that I should just wait and see
All I'm asking for baby, is for you to stand by me
Just like your hand fits inside of a glove
All I want from you is your precious love
For you are my special lady
All I want to know is when something is wrong with my baby
Because when it's all over and the rain stops
I can clearly see your eyes and those lonely tear drops
I want you to clearly see
That when something is wrong you can cry on me
Some look at us and say that our love won't ever grow
But I ask you what do they really know
I never loved a woman the way that I love you
With every beat of my heart, lets me know that this is true
You are my first, my last, my everything
I just want you to know that you make my heart sing
The words that I speak to you are forever true

I just want you to know how much I love you

Come on Girl

Scissors, rocks, paper and stones
Come on girl let's get it on
I'll buy you the world, if I could
Now, come on girl, let me tell you something good
I'll give you chicken, steak and roast
Now, come on girl, let me hold you close
Girl, you know that I can make you feel right
Come on girl, you know I can make your skin tight
Now, you know that you have that special jewel
So come on girl, don't be cruel
You know that you want this special toy
Come on girl, I can be your Mercedes boy
I know you're asking how would you know
Come on girl, you can trust me, because I say so
All I'm asking is for you to give me a chance
Now, you should know something, before this last dance
Come on girl, you know that it's my heart that you can steal
I see, all you think is that I want to show you is my whip appeal
Hey man you don't have to shove
Look, I'm trying to give this woman some of my love

Second Guessing

Girl, let me hold you close
Because it is you that I love the most
Not that there are any others
But I love you more than my sisters and my brothers
All I need with you is just one night
And then I can take away all of your frights
I tell you that you are the one that I seek
You came into my life and I no longer had to creep
I knew that when we first hugged and kissed
That if I let you go you would be truly missed
You look at me and you think that I'm playing
But deep in your heart you know that you should be staying
I can say that there's a chance for me and you
Because, I know that my love I have is so true
You have prayed all of your adult life for a true love
And now that I'm here, you still need a shove
Sometime we ponder and wait too long
And then we end up crying when the other one is gone
You and I both know, that life is too short
So, all of this love I have for you let's not abort
I say that I love you more and more each day
So, let us not let all of this passion slip away

The Problem

In our marriage you wonder why there's not any happiness
Is it because you're afraid to show a little tenderness
Seasons come and seasons are gone
But my love for you is just as strong
When we stood in front of the preacher and I said that I do
And those two words that I said are still true
My love for you has never died
But it's something about the way you make
me feel, deep down inside
I'm trying to get it in your mind and hope you understand
That I'm not trying to push you away to another man
I want you to know that I love you just as much today
And the love that I have for you will never stray
But I refused to be treated this way
But together with you I want to stay
So, is there anything that you want to say

The Answer

The other day when you went away
I looked into the mirror and I heard a voice say
The voice asked me, if you were being treated this way
How much longer will you stay
And then I felt something deep down inside
It was as if part of me had just died
I thought that the love that I wanted was
on the other side of the world
And I fail to realize that you were my true pearl
I know that I can be a little rough around the edges
But just like I take the clippers and I prune the hedges
Look, I really don't know what I'm saying
But until now it was like I was just playing
The thought of me losing you
It's like me catching a case of the flu
I just want to be your man
And I make this promise, that I will do all that I can
I'm willing to go every step above
To let you know that you are truly loved
I want to keep you in my life at all cost
And I don't want you to be the love that I lost

The Reply

I just want to be your wife
I don't want you to feel like I want you out of your life
I don't want you to jump through any hoops, to push or shove
All I want and need is to feel your love
All I need to know is where you stand
And are you willing to stay here and be my man
If you're willing to stay here and walk through the fire
I can assure you that I can fulfill your deepest desire
Because my love for you is true devotion
Now, come on my love let's put this love into motion

Leaving You

Why must I feel like I have to do wrong
Just to make our love carry on
I feel like I have lost you
I thought that our love would forever be true
You say that you're not happy and you want a baby
But I say that I just want you to be my lady
You say that our love has lost its fire
But I say it's you who have lost your desire
When I touch you, you say that it's not the same
But last night when we made love, you
wouldn't even call out my name
You tell me that I don't have to cry
But when I do you still don't even try
You say that in your words I need to trust
But I say that when we sleep together it's just lust
In my heart, I know that there is another
And I refuse to stay here and be your part-time lover

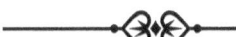

My Wife

When I hold your hand and I'm with you
I know in my heart that our love is true
Other women try to take me away
But I know that this is where I want to stay
You're always giving me something that I can feel
And you make me feel like I'm twenty-one still
At night when my mind is wondering and I can't sleep
You're quick to give me good loving to help me keep
Your friends say that the love we have is something in the past
They're quick to say that our love will never last
I say that they just want to see you go
But the love that we have for each other,
they will never know
Now, when I reach and we're holding hands
I know in my heart that I want to be your husband

The Chase

From the moment that I looked into your eyes
Your beauty, your smile, and your lips just hypnotized
I tried to think of some words to say
But it was like they just left my mind and went away
But now that you lay next to me
The words seem to come and flow efficiently
We have had so much fun with our courtship
Not once have our friendship taken a dip
So, this is why I'm so confused
When you say that I make you feel like you're being used
I've done all that I can to show you that my feelings are true
But yet you're still saying that I using you
I tell you that you're the apple of my eye
So, if I have to win your love back, I'm willing to try
I want you to know that you are my best friend
And there is no way that I want what we have to end

Now, you say that you love me too
So, what is it that you want me to do
Ok, you're tired of living only as friends
You say that you feel like, you're living in sin
I forever want you to stay in my life
For this reason, I'm asking you to be my wife
I guess now it's time for me to take this ring out of my pocket
Wow, looks like you've just stuck your finger into a socket
You have such a glow upon your face
So, I guess this will be the end of my chase

You Say

You told your mother that you will never love again
You say that you don't even want a special friend
You say that you feel like such a jerk
For walking in with your eyes closed and getting hurt
You say that most of the time you feel like staying home
You say that all you want is to be left alone
You say that falling in love again will never be on your plate
You say if another man approaches you, he will meet a closed gate

Momma

Baby, right now you're hurt and your heart is beating fast
I'm here to tell you that this feeling will pass
And there is no reason to just close your door

Because the first time you were in love your heart has hit the floor
I'm telling you that things are not as bad as they seem
And one day it will feel like one bad dream
Sometime we need to go through some hurt and pain
So, that we know it's so much more to be gained
So, don't let one broken heart make you want to stop
Because you know what they say, the cream always raises to the top

The Wrong One

I want you and I want you to stay
I'm not interested in the little games you want to play
I want you to know that I'm the man
And I'm the one who make all of the plans
I'm top cat and you're the mouse
And I'm the one who wears the pants in this house
And you better not say a word to me
When I come in the house at a quarter past three
When I say roll over and say give me some
You give it to me until I'm done
I don't want you wearing anything fake
Now get on up and go fix my plate

I tell you what, today you can fix your own dinner
Because I'm leaving you for a winner
I stayed here and listened to all of your mess
And now I'm going out to get with the best
Shut up, I'm telling you how I feel
And now I'm going with a man who is for real
I shouldn't have hit you upside your head
I should have just left you looking dumb instead
So, as you watch me walk out that door
You can just pick yourself up off of that floor

Date Night

I come into the bedroom and you want me to stay
Oh boy, isn't so funny how time slips away
We fooled around, we kissed and we hugged
We started on the bed and now we're on the rug
I looked at the clock and it's almost eleven
It seemed like a few minutes ago, it was only just seven
I got up, and got ready and headed to the door
But you grabbed my hand and said,
that you wanted some more
There's no way I leave here and leave you hungry
I don't want you sitting here horny and lonely
I'll call my friend and tell him that I will be late
Because me and my beautiful wife are on a very hot date

Living in The Past

Before I met you, I never use to pray
The funny thing is, I wouldn't have known what to say
I finally just ask the Lord to
make me the man that he wants me to be
To make me the man that he wants to see
You see before I use to pray
I tried to do things my own way
And then you came into my life
And now you are my wife
And I discovered the reason why things didn't work
Because I was still feeling the pain still feeling the hurt
Although my love I have for you is true
I was taking all of my hurt and pain out on you
It wasn't until I stopped trying to handle
things with my own hands
That I finally was able to become your husband

The Creeper

You can't continue to come to me whenever you like
You are the one who decided to get married and have a wife
You once said that you always wanted to be with me
But now you're married to her and starting a family
But still you want to sneak over here and creep
But you need to stay over there where you sleep
So, don't come over here, bringing me presents
and trying to be kind
I mean you're still coming over here and giving me
those same old tired lines
While you're at home loving on your wife
You want me here all alone waiting on you
with my same old life
You are the one who walked out and left me all alone
And then you ran to her and started a new home
You use to tell me that I was so fine
I can see now, that all you wanted was some of this behind
So, now when you go out looking for some behind to seek
You can just pass on by and go elsewhere to creep

Infatuated

I simply thought that it was infatuation
When I used to see you in my imagination
I used to think about you from head to toe
This is no line; this is the truth I hope you know
From your brown skin to your soft silk hair
I'm not a shame for you to know how much I care
I look into your eyes so big and round
I can't hear anyone else I can't hear a sound
Your lips look as soft as the clouds above
They remind me of two precious doves
I look at you and try to stay sane
Because as of yet, I don't even know your name
How can I feel for you the way that I do
I do not know the answer, I don't have a clue
I talk about you to all my friends
They tell me that I'm just dreaming, dreaming all over again
I don't know what to do what to say
Maybe one day as I'm walking you will simply just pass my way

The Commitment

Come on girl take my hand
Let me lead you to the promise land
As soon as my feet had hit the ground
I knew that it was true love that I had found
Into your eyes I took one look
And that one look was all that it took
Your friends and my friends tell us not to rush
But I say, that it's our hearts that we should trust
My momma told me to take my time young man
But when I do it's like running in the sand

I don't want any one-night stand
I want someone who is willing to be my husband
You might be looking at me as a steal
But I'm looking for a man who is for real
A man that I can really trust
And not a man who is just thinking about lust
I'm not just looking for a good time and having fun
Because at my mom's house I have my son
So, if you're ready for a complete family
I guess I can give you my number, and you can call on me
And before I let you put a ring on my hand
I have to know if you're ready to be a husband

Part-Time Lover

When we first met you were my part-time lover
But now I don't want you out of my site, there is no other
Because now when I call your name
Something inside of me doesn't feel the same
I thought we would just pass like two ships in the night
But as of now I don't want to let you out of my sight
I thought that I would just be happy just playing the field
But now I can see that you're the real deal
And now when I go to bed at night and don't hear
You voice on the phone
I just lay in my bed feeling all alone
How can a man treat such a precious dove
As if she was nothing but a part-time love
So, as I'm ready to bend down on my knees
I'm asking if you would do the honor and marry me

Let Me Be the Fool

My family keeps telling me that it takes a fool to fall in love
But then I discovered that true love comes from above
And now I know what true love is, I think
Because whenever you leave me my heart starts to sink
And now I can say that I love you so
And I never ever want to see you go
Some are saying that I'm falling too easy
But I feel just like George Jefferson loving his "Weezy"
And if you still don't understand
All I'm saying is that I forever want to be your man

Your Touch

When you touch me
It feels like I can' t see
The stars seem to fall from the sky
And there's a sparkle in my eye
My heart feels like it starts to sink
And now I can't even sleep a wink
I forget about my friends; I forget about them all
Because, I sit patiently at home, just waiting for your call
And when you grab and kiss me, I get weak in the knees
And I want to ask for more, so more please
Sometime I often wonder, what have you done
Whatever it is please don't stop, because it is a lot of fun
When you touch me, I feel like I'm holding my Teddy bear
And I don't have a worry in the world not even a care
I used to just think about having lots and lots of money
But now all I think about is you, isn't that funny
I know that I want to be with you oh so much
Isn't it so funny, that this can happen with just your touch

Hold On

Girl, let me hold you on to you tight
I promise that I will treat you right
You said that you just wanted to have an affair
But I'm going to show you, that you really care
You said that you just wanted a one-night stand
But I say that I'm going to be your man
You said that what we're doing was no big deal
But I say, that you know that what you're feeling is for real
If what you're feeling is not for real, then
why don't get out of my bed
But how come you get closer and kiss me instead
You said that falling in love just doesn't feel right
I say, come on girl and let me take away all of your fright
You said that the last man that said this told you a lie
So, you're just going to push me away and not even try
You say that all I want to do is to have sex with you
We don't have to have sex, because my feelings are true
You say that the last guy caused you so much hurt and so much pain
And you say that you never go through that again
I'm willing to take my time, I willing to take it slow
Because my love for you is true, I want you to know
I never want you to hurt again
To prove my point, I want us to start off as friends
You lay your head on my chest and you start to cry
And when you're finished, I'll dry your eye
I tell you what, let's go into the other room
Because we're laying here in this bed, way too soon
As long as I've been watching you
I don't want to mess this up by doing the do

That's all I want to do is to put a smile upon you face
Until all of the sadness is gone, I don't want to see a trace
Once again, I say, let me hold you tight
And I will chase away all of your frights

Fine China

I tell you that there can be nothing finer
Then my most precious china
You can be out on display, for others to see
But they better know, that you are with me
The way you do your nails, toes and hair
Makes all the other men want to look and stare
You look as sweet as honey made by a bee
But once again those brothers better know that you are with me
They can see that you're sexy and fine
But I tell you this, they had better not cross the line
But if one should get brave enough and try to touch
He will soon find his throat in my clutch
I know that there's nothing finer
Then the one on my arm, my fine china

Taking Too Long

When I'm lying in the bed at night and I'm dreaming
My life somehow takes on a new meaning
And just like a flower when it's in full bloom
The sun seems to come up way too soon
And then I wake up to see
That you're not here with me
I hurry up and pick up the phone to give you a call
And just the sound of your voice calms it all
And then you tell me to hurry back home
That you're so tire of being all alone
I'll be on the two o'clock flight
But I'll still won't be there until tonight
I can't begin to say how much I want to be with you
And then you tell me that you miss me too
I just want to hold you and kiss your lips
I'm getting tired of all of these business trips
You tell me that I don't have to worry about you
Because there's no one else that can do the things that I do
I guess that is the reason that I love you

The Way You Make Me Feel

You have put something in my heart
And I should have known it from the start
Can a candle burn without the flame?
Nor without you my life will never be the same
Marriage life I'm willing to try
Because being together is better, you can't deny
Without any words, can a book be a book
I'm just like a fish in the water and you have me hooked
Would there be any honey without the honey bee?
I'm trying to tell you that I want you here with me
On my face I use to wear a frown
But when I met you, you turned it upside down
Being with me, is it so hard
Because with you I never want us to part
From the moment that you came into my life
I knew right then that I wanted you for my wife
So, just like Marvin Gaye sings his song
Come on girl, let's get it on

Sealed with a Kiss

How can I express the way I really feel
Without making this a big deal
The thoughts of you warm up my darkest nights
You take away my biggest frights
You are as soft as the clouds above
It would be so easy for anyone to fall in love
But you know and I know that this may not be
But who knows we should just wait and see
Your eyes are like a burning fire
They can ignite my deepest desire
We were supposed to have passed like two ships in the night
But now I don't want to let you out of my sight
I hope that this poem doesn't push you away
Because friends and more I want to always stay
I pray that this poem lets you know how I feel
And now with a kiss I seal

Leave Me Alone

Why do I want to be with you
Do you know the reason do you have clue
When I'm with you I'm treated like a disease
Yet I continue to beg I continue to plead
You say that your love for me is true
But yet I really don't know what to do
My feelings for you I try so hard to hide
But you see right through me, you see deep inside
Girl if you could only feel what I feel
Then you would know that my love for you is real
You think the words that I say are just lines
You may think all I want to do is bump and grind
Although my feelings for you are strong
I will not stay here and let you treat me so wrong
So, when I close the door and tell you bye
You can simply walk out and continue to hold your head up high

Precious Love

As the sun comes up to shine
I thank the Lord every day that you are mine
They say that you can mail order a bride
I'm glad to say that I didn't have to because
you came from deep down inside
The day that I met you I didn't have a clue
That the feelings and love we have would soon be true
When I first looked at your lips, they looked ever so sweet
And now when I look at you the fire in me burns so deep
Just like a dog that loves his bone
I know that our love will carry on
The sun will never cease to shine
Because forever you will be mine
And just like an ornament that hangs from a tree
I know in my heart that we were meant to be

If Only I Knew

Like the wind that blows through the wind chimes
Like the flowers that bloom in the spring time
My love for you will never go
All that it can ever do is to grow
Like the birds that fly against the evening sky
I know that we can make it if we try
Like the wind that tosses the ocean and the sea
I know that I want you here with me
Like the car that races around the track
What I'm trying to tell you, is that I want you back

Evil Thoughts

When I first looked at you, you were so fine
I wished then and there that you were mine
Those thoughts I tried so hard to end
Because you could never be mine, you were with my friend
I don't know how wrong this might seem
But when I sleep at night, you're often in my dreams
I see us walking on the beach in the sand
I see us walking together, holding each other's hand
When I see you two laughing and having fun
I want to tell so bad, all of the things that he has done
But I won't, I will keep them to myself
I will leave that to tell for someone else
Because the feelings that I have for
you, I don't know if I can trust
Are they feelings of love, or are they just feelings of lust
I look at your body, I look at your curves
I wonder how it would be if you were my girl

Selfish

When I think of myself of old
I can understand why you would say that I'm ruthless and cold
I never put thought into anyone else
Because all that I ever cared about was myself
True enough, I've met a man and he loved me
He loved me so much that wanted to start a family
He was the man that I wanted in my life
I wanted him, but not enough to stay his wife
He gave me what I wanted, which was a family
But, at that time that wasn't enough for me
So, I took the easiest route, I took the easiest course
I said that I was unhappy, and I asked for a divorce
And now that time has past
I often wish that our marriage would have lasted
He has moved on with his life
And now he's married and has a new wife
I have only one wish
And some of you might think that I'm selfish
My wish is that he is as happy as he can be
At least as far as I can see
But my only wish is, that he would have only have waited for me

Puppy Love

You say that you thought that we would always be together
I too thought that you would always be my lady
But then you went off to college and had a baby
Some of the guys thought that I should have been mad
Naw, I just found out that you weren't the girl I thought I had
And now when I think about it, we were both young
We were just enjoying life and having fun
And now that time has passed
I can't help to wonder, if our relationship would have lasted
We both thought that the feelings we had were true
But I guess we both had a lot of growing up to do
Now that I have moved on with my life
I've settled down with my wife
I can look back over the things that we did
And I can honestly say that we were both just kids
And I can thank the heavens up above
For this thing that they call puppy love

Living in Fear

Every time you would get close, I would push you away
But then I would turn around and want you to stay
You seem like you were pouring your heart out to me
It seemed like you really wanted to start a family
But when I saw the love that you had for me
I ran away before it fully developed, before we could see
I guess you got tired of this off and on
Because I woke up one day and you were gone
It's not your fault, you're not to blame
It is I as a man who should be ashamed

Let's Talk

When I first saw this boy, I thought he was so fine
I just knew that I had to make him mine
He was just fifteen
But I thought I could be his pretty little queen
But I was just a student in the sixth grade
And I had perfect grades I made all A's
I made a mistake and told how I feel
But at that time, I thought it was no big deal
He pulled me to the side and whispered I love you
But I didn't realize that he just wanted to do the do
Just remember, that I was just in the sixth grade and only eleven
He told me to meet him at his house around about seven
I told my mom that I was going to my friend's
And from that very moment on all of my innocence's would end
From the moment I got there, he started to kiss and hug
Then he put his hand in my pants and he started to rub
Before I could tell him stop
I felt my pants and my underwear drop
He told me to turn around and to bend over
I then felt his hands up on my shoulder
Which I thought was very strange
And then all of a sudden, I felt so much pain
I wanted to run, I wanted to hide
But then it felt like something was pouring in me, deep down inside
And then he pulled out and ran away
I didn't know if I should leave or if I should stay
I slowly stood up and fixed my clothes
I had tears down my face and snot running out of my nose
I slowly walked home, thinking who can I tell

I thought, here I am having sex, I'm not even twelve
Three months would go by and I'm starting to show
I thought, can I keep this from my mom, or does she already know
I tried to call him and tell him what he had done
But he said that he would call me back,
that he was outside having fun
So, I decided to wait by the phone
I thought, he would call me back that it wouldn't take too long
I came to realize that all his sweet words weren't true
I was getting beside myself; I didn't know what to do
My mom called out, we're going for a float
I started to run out the door, and I forgot my coat
I tried to turn around, before she could see
But she wasn't fooled, she was there waiting for me
She said that it was hard enough raising us three
And that she would help, but this baby would depend me
Months seemed to drag by, and then it was September
Something happened then, something that
I would always remember
I thought, before I could grow up and become a lady
I was going to the hospital to have my own baby
But as you can see
I didn't let having you stop me
I went back to school and I still made all A's
I wasn't going to work for any minimum wage
And now for the man that's called your dad
I guess I should be angry, I should be mad
But I can't be mad at him, and not at me too
Because I realize that there are consequences
for the things that we do
It's just some of us learn from the things that we did
And some of us don't, I guess this is why he has eleven kids
So, before you find yourself starting an early family
I want you to know that you can always talk to me

Use Your Head

You told me that us sleeping together was no big deal
Because for several years now, you've been on the pill
You said that a condom I didn't have to wear
That I could come on in without a care
But now I'm standing here with this frown
Because you fail to tell me that you often slept around
I had to go to the doctors for a second trip
Because my little man has continued to drip
He told me that he wanted to run some
more test, so that he could see
If I could have possibly contracted HIV
And now you're standing here looking all ashamed
But to be honest I have to say, that you're not all the blame
Hold on, before you say, what I think you're going to say
I know before I slept with you, I wasn't this way
Well, I was just telling you so that you could know
But if you would excuse me, I better go

One Night Will Not Do

I was supposed to hold you for only night
But for some reason, in my heart that just didn't feel right
From the moment that you sunk into my arms
I wanted to keep you and fill you with all of my charm
So, then I knew
That one night with you, just simply would not do
From the time that we first kissed
I knew that if you left, you would be sorely missed
And yet you still choose to walk away
I guess this is the silly game that you choose to play
You came into my life and you loved me down
And now all of a sudden you want to sleep around
I just knew that you were here to stay
But yet when we finished, you still got up and walked away
Your leaving hurts like getting hit by a truck
But I guess all that you wanted was to get stuck

Magic Moment

From your beautiful smile to your elegant style
From your jazzy talk to your sexy walk
You are so lovely to me
You are someone I would love to wake and see
From the first time I saw you
I knew my feelings were true
You look like an angel from above
An angel that was sent to share my love
When we are together, we always share a laugh or two
Let us not forget the other things we love to do
We laugh and play
Feeling like young we will always stay
I don't think there's anything wrong
By us having these feelings so strong
Sitting here looking at you with little to say
I hope that these feelings we have will always stay

They Say

They tell me to wait for love, what's the rush
Because if I move too fast, my heart can get crushed
Just because you tell me that you love me
They tell me to slow down and wait and see
My heart seems to skip a beat, when you touch my hand
They say for me to hold up, you just might have another man
I love it when we hug and kiss
But they say, move too fast I'll be taking a risk
I enjoy you so much, I want to take you home
But they say, that if I do it could be very wrong
With you I feel like I could start a family
Once again, they say, that I should just wait and see
With you I just want to build my house
They say, that there is no way I should want you for my spouse
With you I feel like our love is true
They say, that I should not fall in love with you
But before I turn around and let you go
Maybe you should just open up and tell me what is
it that they are supposed to know

Muddy Love

When I look at you my heart starts to flutter
But yet you can stand there and accuse me of another
How can you love me if there is no trust
So, when we sleep together, I guess it's all just lust
But when I walk out the door and I try to leave
You run behind me you beg and you plead
Do you know what love is, do you even care to know
Love is not pretend love is not just for show
When you can let scripture sink into your heart
Maybe then we can have a new life we get a fresh start
I said that I love you and I really do
But I can't keep putting up with what you're putting me through
I had to look in the mirror and look at myself
I had to stop looking around and blaming everyone else
Then I fell on the floor and I began to plead
I asked the Lord to step in, and make me
And my eyes were opened and I was able to see
The blame wasn't on everyone else the blame was on me

Slow Down

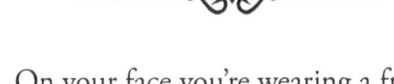

On your face you're wearing a frown
Simply for the fact I asked you to slow down
Of course, I don't want you to leave
Can you find this in your heart to believe
I just want us to take it slow
You know that I don't want you to go
Yes, it's because I've been hurt before
Because we made love, he got up, and walked out the door
If you love me like you say, what's the rush
I'm just trying not to get my heart crushed
You say that you don't buy a car without a test
Well, you just have to believe me,
when I say that I am the best
I really don't know why I'm asking you to stay
You can just get on up and be on your way
Because you have just let me know up front
That it's to sleep with me and sex is all you want
Don't even try to be sweet and kind
Because now I know exactly what's on your mind
So, there's no way in hell that I'll let you stay
You can get on up and be on your way

Enjoying Love

Remembering when we first met, we tried to impress
We looked so sharp we looked your best
At night on the phone we would often stay
Even if we didn't have any words or we didn't know what to say
Before she got in the car you would open the door
It wasn't so hard it wasn't a chore
When you walked anywhere you would hold her hand
Even if you were just waiting in line at the concession stand
Those three words you tried not to say
But for some reason they came out anyway
When you looked into her eyes your heart started to melt
It was like you were just punched in your gut right above your belt
With her, you wanted to go everywhere
What about your friends, oh, you didn't even care
Now as the day comes to an end and you must be going
You anxiously wait for the next day for the early morning

My Queen

When a man finds a good wife
He can forget all about his old life
Those words are not how they might seem
Those words are meant to be a good thing
He turns from the things that he used to do
Because of the love that he has for you
The ones he used to talk to, now he can forsake all others
Because his wife he now has is closer than his mother
When he's low and filling down
His wife can say one word and bring him back around
His wife will do all that she can
But you must always remember to be the man
Not that you just stand around and pump your chest
But in your house, you must demonstrate to the rest
When it comes to praising God, you lead the way
You just don't go to church on a special day
The love that you have for her, you must learn to show
So, that there will be no doubt in her
mind, and she will always know

Forever Mine

The flowers in your meadow are in full bloom
Your search for love will be coming soon
You will soon be getting a different appetite
One that will sometime not allow you to sleep at night
You were like a babe crying in the woods
I would have optioned to keep you that way, if I could
The flowers that once only bloomed on your tree
They kept you hungry, hungry only for me
But now your fruit are starting to appear
And I can no longer just keep you near
My heart often thinks of the times
Where it was only my arms that you wished to find
It was once that I gave you much delight
I was the one who chased away your darkest frights
But now the taste of your fruit is turning sweet
And I know that forever with me I can no longer keep
So, just like your river has changed it flow
I know in my heart that I must be letting go
But from this time and until the end of the world
You will forever be daddy's little girl
I love you

Stay Calm

Just like the waves that are toss in the ocean
I fill like our love is just going through the motions
Don't take it so light when I say that I love you
Those words that I so often spoke are still true
But somewhere in my mind I still want to be free
I'm trying to explain this to you, don't you see
When you ask me, where am I about to go
I would have told you if I wanted you to know
Sometime I just want to be all by myself
And no not because there's anyone else
I might just want some time to think
And no, I really don't want our marriage to sink
When you leave the house, and you say
that you're running some errands
I don't say anything but it's not like I'm not caring
Maybe I should just let you know how I feel
But I want you to know that I do love you still
Our marriage has come a very long way
And in it I do want us to stay
Just like a boat on the calm blue sea
I truly know that this is where I want to be

Cougar

If I told you that I was about to go
What would you do, do you even know
You tell me all of the time that you really care
But the words that you speak, just floats into thin air
When we first got together many years ago, you said to me
You said that you were ready to settle down and start a family
So, If I walk out that door and through that gate
Would you be sad with a tear in your eye, or would you celebrate
Until you realized that I'm really gone
And then maybe in your heart you know that you're wrong
I gave you the best years of my life
I treated you like a husband was supposed to treat his wife
After all the years together, you now want to show your hand
And now you want to leave me for a much younger man
You ask me why do I laugh, what's so funny
Why can't you see that he wants only your money
You say that I'm old and I can't do what I use to do
Now, those words that you speak are probably true
So, the only thing that I have left to say is I give you my best
And I wish the both of you a lot of happiness

My Love

When it's dark outside and there's not any light
I can't help but to hope for a rainy night
When we are together there is no other
But I can't stand it when you're my distant lover
Every time that you come around
I don't want to stop until I love you down
I don't have to make love to you to know that you're my girl
But when I do make love, I want to rock your world
I truly hate it when you go away
I know in my heart that you won't let your love stray
Even on the darkest night, you're my shining star
In the morning and at night, I'll always
love you the way you are
And when the clouds float across the sky
I still can see the sparkles in your eye

Saying Good-Bye

I thought that together we would always stay
I never dreamed about one of us passing away
But just like the flowers that bloom in June
I know in my heart that I will see you soon
My love for you will never die
But I'm going to continue with my life, I won't lie
I will remember the good times that we had
And there will always be the times when I'm sad
If not for you there's no telling where I'll be
And without you I would not have this family
You gave me ambition and you gave me a shove
But most of all you gave me all of your love

Forgotten Time

Welcome to the room that time has forgot
Oh, I'm sorry did I put you on the spot
In here we use to laugh, love and play our games
But since we've gotten married nothing has been the same
They say that marriage is supposed to be love and happiness
So, can you tell me why our target is often missed
Our lives could be the best
If you would simply stop listening to all of the rest
Your friends are always telling you what they would do
There's one thing to remember, and that is they're not you
I've done all I can, I've done my best
But yet you continue to listen to the rest
Do they mean that much to you, please let me know
Because if they do, then just say so
And I won't stand in the way, I will just let you go
But when you go, don't look back
I want you to take all of your clothes that you can pack
There will be hurt, there will be pain
But overall, I feel like I'll be the one who'll gain

The Last Stains

The stains on my pillow throughout the years
Are examples of all of my blood, sweat and tears
For years I've tried to be a good wife
But you thought that I didn't know about your double life
At home you acted like you loved me
But out there you got with all the women that you could see
You told me that you were going with the boys to have some fun
But what about all the money that you spent on the condoms
I did my best to be sexy, I did all that I could
In hoped that you would have remembered
that I'm your woman, I wished that you would
I lay in the bed at night hoping that you would see
That I'm lying here wanted some love, wanting you in me
I have stayed here patiently trying to be a good wife
But now all I have to say is that I too want to have a life
You say that you want me to stay, that you don't want me to leave
But I say that this was the last straw, when you gave me this disease

Letting Go

My love for you will forever be true
I may not have the words or know what to do
I want you to rest and know that it is not you
I don't want tears in your eyes I don't you to be blue
I know that I have to learn to love myself
Before I can fully be in love with someone else
I walk through this life with such a heavy heart
Wondering what must I do to get a fresh start
A voice tells me that I must first let go of the past
That I am the one that's allowing the hurt and pain to last
How can I do this how can I start
You can do this by first opening up your heart
You can do this with ease you just might discover
It's like walking, just put one foot in front of the other
How can I do this it's not that easy for me
You must picture it in your mind you must want to be free
You have it in your mind and you hear what I say
Now just open up your mouth and start to pray

Testing Times

On my face the rain started to fall
While I sat in the park waiting for you call
From the moment that my feet hit the floor
I now realize why you left out that door
I wasn't the man that you wanted me to be
But I know that I can change can't you wait to see
Just like fish live in the sea
I know that our love is meant to be
When I lay down and close my eyes at night
I see you leaving which is my biggest fright
I love the way that you comb your hair
I use to stand behind you and just stare
When we look at each other and our lips start to touch
I want you to know that you mean so much
So, as we walk together hand in hand
I can prove to you that I am the man
My phone starts to ring and I answer the call
Now I see that you still love me after all

My Undying Love

My true love for you may be hard to express
But with these few words I will do my best
With each tear that falls, I promise you that I
will be there through it all
Just like the stars that are in the sky
My love for you will never die
The beauty that you have I will always see, it
doesn't matter what difference may come or how old we maybe
For all of the things done for all of your headaches,
I just want you to know how much I appreciate
Saying I love you is oh so true, but just saying those three words
Just simply will not do

Two in Love

When a man loves a woman, he'll give her everything
On her finger he will even place a ring
When a woman loves a man, she won't ask for it all
Should would even lift him up and help him when he falls
When a man loves a woman, he's quick to represent
Because he knows that this woman of his is heaven sent
When a woman loves a man, she'll dress in her best
Because she knows that it's him that she wants to impress
When a man loves a woman, he'll learn to be kind
He'll learn to leave all of his bad habits behind
When a woman loves a man, she might lose a friend
Because she's knows that some of her old relationships has to end

The Definition of Love

Love is precious love is blind
In my eyes you will always be fine
Love is precious love is blind
In my eyes you will always be mine
Just like the wild flowers that bloom in June
I know in my heart we will be married soon
Love is precious love is blind
Love will always be right on time
Just like the birds that fly through the air
Love is often given with much care
Love is precious love is blind
Love is sweet love is divine
Love is precious love is blind
When you give love, it is given back, and all is fine
Just saying those three words, just simply will not do
You must feel them in your heart and show them too
Love is precious love is blind
Love is one of those words that is hard to define

My Mind Playing Tricks

My mind tells me that you are the real thing
But yet my heart won't let me pull the string
My mind loves everything about you
But my heart says that your love isn't true
I say in my mind, but he's so fine
But my heart tells me that you will never be mine
My mind loves the way that you make me feel
But without sex, would you be here still
I have to learn to just say no
And then maybe your true feelings will show
Because every time that you come around
All you ever want to do is to love me down
You never ever want to take me anywhere
I guess that should tell me that you really don't care
My mind tells me that I shouldn't leave you alone
But my heart says that I should have been long gone
My mind tells me that I should ask you to stay
But my heart tells me to hurry and push you away
My heart tells me that I must learn to be strong
That I must first learn to be happy all alone
My heart tells me that having a man isn't a must
That it's my heart that I have to learn to trust
My heart says that it's not love that I seek
It's just I often give in when my body gets weak
My heart says to myself I must learn to say no
And then and only then will I start to grow
My heart says how can I find the man that I can trust

When all I ever do is to keep giving in to lust

What Do You Want

You thought that you had a man that you could trust
But he was all about greed, he was all about lust
And now he has left you in the dust
You go around talking about its love or bust
The man comes and shows you love
But you push him away, you give him the shove
He took you to the beach, he took you to the cove
But yet you still left him standing out in the cold
You say that he is too nice and kind
You don't know what love is, how can you be so blind
Because he treated you like a lady, you say that he's weak
What are you looking for, what do you seek
You say that you want a man with the right stuff
What, a man that will treat you wrong,
a man that will treat you rough
Now you're back with the man that was filled with greed and lust
So, it's not the man but it's you that you don't trust

My Promise

The sun shines and the rain falls
And I promise that I will love you through it all
When I say that I do
My promise to you will always be true
When we're older and we start a family
The beauty that you now have I will always see
When we're standing there and we're holding hands
I want you to know that I will always be your husband
You will always be my girl
And I will always be in your world
Time will past and we might have a child or two
But we must remember the things that we love to do
There can be nothing worse
Than to forget the love that we had at first
I want you to forever feel the love that's in my heart
As we stand her getting this new start

What's Happening

Every time I close my eyes
I dream about your bodacious thighs
Every time I take a sip
I think about your luscious lips
Every time I see the clouds up above
I think about how we use to make love
It's so funny, that before we tied the knot
You use to drop it like it was hot
I guess now you think that our relationship is old
Your love is just like a faucet that's stuck on cold
Whenever I try to hold you tight
You tell me not right now, not tonight
I try to show you that I love you
But your actions push me away, like I have the flu
Where did it go, where is the sex appeal
Sometime I wonder if your love for me is for real
With your body you refuse to show
Since I'm your husband, shouldn't your body I know
Maybe I should just stop, maybe I shouldn't try
It often makes me think if there's another guy
Do you want my love, do you want me to stay
Maybe I should just pack my bags and go away
If this is not what you want just say so
There will be hurt but then we'll both know

All the Same

The streets for our love go both ways
It doesn't matter if they're dirt, gravel or paved
Your eyes are like two dark pearls
That were meant to share my world
Your lips are as precious as doves
That whisper words of sweet love
And the strength of your hands tells me
that you are truly my man
When we are together and you hold me tight
You remove all of my tension all of my fright
Just like the flames fuels the fire
You fill me up with all of your desire
And just like a child learns to speak
When you're in me you're oh so deep
We go together like two hands in a glove
Two that were meant to share each other's love
Just like the sun shines, there will be the rain
But I promise you that I will love you all the same

What A Relief

When I looked at you from across the room
I knew then and there you would be mine soon
But then I saw you with another man
He held you close, he held your hand
I asked my Lord how could this be
I knew in my heart that you were
supposed to be with me
When we looked into each other's eyes
It was like we were two clouds just
floating in the blue skies
But now that I see you with
him, my heart starts to sink
I guess, I'll just go to the bar and
have another drink
But how could this be, I see you walking my way
I hope that you don't stop, because, I will want you to stay
You say hello, and I ask you if there is another
You say, oh him, you must have seen me talking to my brother
We start to talk and the conversation gets good
Things are going great, just like they should
I ask you if you have any other plans
Then you reach over and grab my hand
My heart starts to beat it starts to pound
I couldn't hear anything else, I couldn't hear a sound
I looked deep into your eyes, I looked in your face
You asked me, do you want to go to a quieter place
You holding my hand we walked across the floor
I thought we we're going to stop, but we walked out the door
You asked me did I take a taxi or did I drive

But then you say, I saw you when you first arrived
You tell me, I wanted to make sure that you were by yourself
Make sure that you weren't meeting someone else
I told my brother that you were the man for me
He said, that I should just slow do and wait to see
I am so glad that I waited and met you
So, where do we go from here what do we do

Another Lonely Night

Here I am spending another lonely night
I thought you would be here to hold me tight
I thought since my feelings were so strong
That you would never think of treating me wrong
I gave you all of the love that I had
But yet I still lay here feeling empty and sad
I even got up and made you breakfast in bed
When I should have been kicking you out instead
I guess to you this was just another lustful affair
And here I am thinking that you really care
One day you too will be all alone
Then and only then will you want to make a home
But until then I lay here burning with desire
Without your love to quench my fire
You might think that here I will always be
That I'm waiting for you to decide,
that you want to be with me
Just like the crow when it caws
You not being here tonight, is the last straw

Just Love

I never ever want to give you up
It will be like the coffee without the cup
It will be like having the sun without the shine
Because in my heart it will feel like you were never mine
Just like the dew that settles on the morning grass
I want our love to forever last
When darkness falls and I can't see
I feel so much better knowing that you are with me
We're like two sets of hands inside of gloves
We were meant to share this precious love
Just like you plant a seed and watch it grow
Our love is true, I want you to know
If I lose you, I can't say that my world would end
But I would know that I've lost my true love and my best friend

Just My imagination

I truly thought it was just my imagination
When I saw that my Lord had made such a beautiful creation
From your beautiful eyes to your sexy curves
I'm so glad that you were placed in my world
When I look at how you stand, you look so sweet
It's enough to make my heart skip a beat
From the bottom of your feet to the tip of your hair
Makes me just want to look at you, makes me want to stare
Your eyes shine like polished glass
Which lets me know that you're in a higher class
And when you smile, I look at your pearly whites
They are so bright, they can even block the sun light
And when I look at your personality
I know that I want this marriage to become a reality

Listen to What I Say

Who cares about what the world and people say
I'm going to love you anyway
Because in my mind you will always be fine
And in my heart, you will always be mine
I know that you're not the person that you used to be
But in my eyes, you will always be beautiful to me
I remember the walks where we used to walk hand in hand
You are my woman and I'm your man
How we used to walk by and the guys used to stare
But as long as they didn't touch, I didn't even care
Today a lot of people might find it strange
That my love for you has never changed
Am I not supposed to love you, because you're not the same
Time plays tricks on everyone and we're not to blame
You're still the sugar in my cup of coffee
And forever want you with me

Can't Trust Myself

I thought that I was speaking words that I can trust
But it turned out that I was just speaking words of lust
When I said that I wanted us to start a family
I guess I just wanted you to lay down with me
When I told you that I loved you
I guess I just wanted to do the do
I know that you're a really good man
And someday you're going to make
some woman a good husband
So, when we're finished, I'll just get up and walk away
Please don't complicate matters by asking me to stay
My words that I speak are seldom true
But I feel like I could learn to love you
I guess it's going to take me seeing you with someone else
For me to realize that I should have kept you for myself
One day my selfishness will cause me to cry
And there will be no one there to help dry my eye
How can I learn to love if there's no trust
I guess until I do, I'll just keep on living in lust

Love Gone

Since I lost my baby
I find myself second guessing and thinking maybe
Maybe I should get with this one
Maybe I should just have some fun
I found my life going down the drain
Most of the time, I just wish that it would rain
Because then the tears that are upon my face
They won't leave a trail they won't leave a trace
Summer is now gone
And fall seems to be coming on
The times of sadness are here
I must learn to have some pep, must
learn to have some cheer
I'm still sitting here wondering, why did she leave me
I thought that we were one big happy family
I guess being in love, it really takes two
But now that she's gone, I don't know what to do
But she did say that she loved me
I guess I should have taken the time and waited to see

I'm I Dreaming

When I lay down to sleep, I often see you in my dreams
But I never met you, I wonder what does this mean
You're so beautiful to me, you have everything that I like
But when I wake, I try to think of you, it's like I lose my sight
I want to hurry and go back to sleep
Because the thought of you, I want to always keep
When I go to work it's hard for me to concentrate
And when I go to lunch, I can't help but to
see your face in my dinner plate
A picture of you in my mind I want to see clear
But will there be a day when I'll be able to hold you near
When I lay down at night, my heart starts to skip a beat
With the anticipation that I will see you in my sleep
I tossed and turned all night long
But my thought of you wasn't there, it was gone
But the thought of you seemed so real
I guess I just have to believe and wait for the real deal

Time Will Tell

When I first met you, I thought you were my one and only
But now that I'm with you, how come I'm still lonely
When we first met, we thought that this
were how things were meant to be
But we should have taken our time, so that we could really see
We rushed in because we thought that it was
our feelings that we could trust
But it turns out that our feelings might
have been based on just lust
But when you touched me, you made me feel
like no one else ever could
Our feelings were so deep, you felt so good
I thought that I never ever wanted to see you go
But you had no substance, you were just all show
But when it's time for you to leave, time for you to be dismissed
I ran back into your arms, and greeted you with a kiss
My friends and my mind are telling me too let you go
But my heart is saying not to do so
But now that time has passed
I never would have thought that our love would have lasted
I'm glad that you stayed here and put up with me
Because now we have such a beautiful family

Forget Me Not

When I am gone
I know that our love will continue on
The sun will not cease to shine
Nor will our love be left behind
I may not be there to dry the tears from your eye
I may not be there to hold you when you cry
Just remember those words that were nice and kind
The words that are stored deep so deep inside of your mind
I know that soon you will get a fresh start
And I know that I will always have a special place in your heart
Again, my face you may never see
So, all that I ask is for you to remember me
So, when you look up at the blue sky above
Think about all the special moments we shared
And think about how you were truly loved

Where Would I Be

I can only imagine where I would be
If my Lord wasn't willing to die upon that tree
They nailed Him up there all stretched out wide
While all of the time he was thinking of me, deep down inside
And then His blood started to drop
But you know, that If He wanted to, He could have made it stop
And then He died, and for the world to know
The heavens itself put on a show
But still his love for me still wasn't finished
He still had to go into hell to show satan
that his powers were diminished
I think back, if He had not done this for me
Only He knows where I would be
When most think of love, they might
think of cupid or little turtle doves
But He gave up His life for me, now that is love
When I think of my Lord all stretch out wide
I get a special feeling, deep down inside
I know that He didn't do this just for me
He did this so, we can all might become his family

Spreading His Love

I ran do the hall and then across the floor
And then I forced open the old wooden door
They said that he was down the hall and to the right
I knew if found him, that I wouldn't let him out of my sight
And then I passed a mirror, and what did I see
I saw Him, and He was on the inside of me
I asked Him, how long has he been there
He answered, I've been here before
your first breathe of air
I asked Him, how long does He plan to stay
He said, Oh, I'll be here until you pass away
And then I saw two birds fly, they were two doves
He said that I chose you to help spread my message of love
I had to ask, why would you choose me
He, answered, there's a lot in you, a lot you can't yet see
How would I know where to start, how would
I know when the time is right
He said, I just want you to get a pen and
paper and start to write
The words that I put on paper, they started to flow
Where are these words coming from, I don't know
He told me to write on every subject matter
He said, to some it will be the Gospel
and some would run and scatter
To some it will come as a relief
And to others, it will test their belief
But over all I want you to share my message of love
Because with me and my father, that's all it's about, up here above

The Peace Within

When I'm with you there's nothing but peace
My worries in this world are the least
Even when I don't see you, you are always by my side
Because I know that for me you hung on that cross and died
Because of the blood you shed, I will never have steal, borrow or beg
I know that when it's all over, and from this earth I'm gone
That you've already prepared a place for me, a new home
My age I will never have to worry, I will never grow old
And the streets that I walk on are made of gold
But I know as long as I'm in this life
I still don't have to worry about the pain, hurt and strife

We Found Each Other

I wasn't supposed to fall in love
I was supposed to be walking away, I was about to shove
But you're the lady in my imagination
The one who had me walking around in frustration
In my life, why did you come so late
But to be honest, I have to say that
you were well worth the wait
Because now when we're walking hand on hand
I can truly say that I'm ready to be your husband
I guess my Lord was waiting on me
To decide that I really wanted a family
I can't begin to tell you how much I've grown
And now I know that my love is strong
When I first use to see you in my imagination
Maybe then, it just might have been infatuation
Because I used to dream about how
we would touch, kiss and hug
You know, how we might start on the
bed and end up on the rug
I can't even begin to tell you how beautiful you are
I know that you are the best catch, the best by far
Your beauty shines even in the darkness of night
And it's even the same in the early morning light
My friends use to tell me that my dream would never come true
But I can smile now, because here I am with you

I know that when I use to close my eyes, I could see your face
And that is one image I use to chase
My girls used to tease me about my fantasy man

They used to tell me, there is no way he's your husband
They told me to just settle for this other guy
I almost gave in, I almost gave him a try
But I stopped it before it had a chance to start
Because something didn't feel right, deep down in my heart
I am so happy that waited on you
Because now I know that our love is true
And now that we know that our love is strong
We should get together and just float on
Now come on boy and hold me close
Because it's your love that I've been wanting the most

www.ingramcontent.com/pod-product-compliance
Lightning Source LLC
Chambersburg PA
CBHW030348100526
44592CB00010B/879